First World War
and Army of Occupation
War Diary
France, Belgium and Germany

32 DIVISION
97 Infantry Brigade
Manchester Regiment
53rd Battalion
1 March 1919 - 4 November 1919

WO95/2404/3

The Naval & Military Press Ltd
www.nmarchive.com
Published in association with The National Archives

Published by

The Naval & Military Press Ltd

Unit 10 Ridgewood Industrial Park,

Uckfield, East Sussex,

TN22 5QE England

Tel: +44 (0) 1825 749494

www.naval-military-press.com

www.nmarchive.com

This diary has been reprinted in facsimile from the original. Any imperfections are inevitably reproduced and the quality may fall short of modern type and cartographic standards.

© **Crown Copyright**
Images reproduced by permission of The National Archives, London, England, 2015.

Contents

Document type	Place/Title	Date From	Date To
Heading	WO95/2404/3		
Heading	Lancashire Division (Late 32nd Divn) 97th Infy Bde (3rd Lancs Infy Bde) 53rd Bn Manchester Regt Mar-Oct 1919		
War Diary	Crowborough	01/03/1919	03/03/1919
War Diary	Dunkirk	04/03/1919	15/03/1919
War Diary	Menden	16/03/1919	01/05/1919
War Diary	Meden In Germany	01/05/1919	24/05/1919
War Diary	Menden	25/05/1919	01/06/1919
War Diary	Germany	21/06/1919	29/06/1919
War Diary		03/06/1919	03/06/1919
War Diary	Germany	01/06/1919	19/06/1919
War Diary		02/06/1919	02/06/1919
War Diary	Birlinghoven	01/07/1919	04/08/1919
War Diary	Hennef	05/08/1919	30/08/1919
War Diary		02/09/1919	02/09/1919
War Diary	Hennef	01/09/1919	24/10/1919
War Diary	Hennef	04/11/1919	04/11/1919

WO 95/24041 3

LANCASHIRE DIVISION
(LATE 32ND DIVN)

97TH INFY BDE (3RD LANCS INFY BDE)

53RD BN MANCHESTER REGT.
MAR - OCT 1919

WAR DIARY
or
INTELLIGENCE SUMMARY.
(Erase heading not required.)

Army Form C. 2118.

Place	Date	Hour	Summary of Events and Information	Remarks and references to Appendices
CROWBOROUGH.	1.3.1919.		53rd (Service)Battn. The Manchester Regt. The Battalion inspected in Hyde Park by H.M.The King at 1430. The Unit formed together with 51st & 52nd Royal Fusiliers, 53rd Liverpool Regt, No 4 Brigade. Officers of the Battalion present. Colonel A.C.Bolton. Major A.G.Hills. Capt: E.J.Lloyd. 2/Lieut. E.P.H.Pugh. "E" Coy: Capt: E.R.Brittain. Capt: J.W.Evatt. Lieut: J.O.Richardson. Lieut: N.W.Sutcliffe. 2/Lt: H.E.Jessup. Capt: H.E.R.Warton. "A" Coy. Capt: J.F.Johnson. Lieut: S.Hammond. 2/Lieut. F.R.Ragg. 2/Lieut. L.Frost. 2/Lieut. E.Brocklehurst. "B" Coy: Captain S.T.Brown. Captain T.M.Cowan. Lieut: F.J.Ward. Lieut. S Keys. Lieut. W.Chapman. 2/Lt: G.Parsons. "D" Coy. Captain A.W.Keeley. Captain R.Shankland. Lieut: D.H.Bowen. 2/Lt: G.H.Ault. 2/Lt: F.Bradley. 2/Lt: F.Cookson. Lieut: & Q.M. W.H.Smith. Capt Duke. (Medical Officer) Orders received on return, for removal of Battalion overseas on March 3rd 1919.	
	2.3.1919.		Battalion engaged in preparations for proceeding overseas.	
	3.3.1919.		Battalion leaves Crowborough in two trains arriving Dover same evening. 4 Sergeants, 3 Corporals, reported from 4th Bn. Border Regt:	

Army Form C. 2118.

WAR DIARY
or
INTELLIGENCE SUMMARY.
(Erase heading not required.)

Instructions regarding War Diaries and Intelligence Summaries are contained in F. S. Regs., Part II. and the Staff Manual respectively. Title pages will be prepared in manuscript.

Place	Date	Hour	Summary of Events and Information	Remarks and references to Appendices
DUNKIRK.	4.3.1919.		Battalion proceeds overseas arriving Dunkirk at 1330. Encamped for the night at No.4.Rest Camp.	
			List of Officers who proceeded overseas:-	
			Colonel A.C.Bolton. "H.Q".	
			Major A.G.Hills.	
			Capt: & Adjt: E.J.Lloyd.	
			Lieut. H.E.Roose.	
			Lieut: & Q.M. W.H.Smith.	
			2/Lieut: E.P.H.Pugh.	
			Captain H.E.R.Warton. "A" Coy.	
			Lieut: J.F.Johnson.	
			Lieut: F.Hammond.	
			2/Lt: W.E.G.Serjeant.	
			2/Lt: L.Frost.	
			2/Lt: L.T.Smith.	
			2/Lt: J.T.Milner.	
			2/Lt: F.R.Ragg.	
			Captain S.T.Brown. "B" Coy.	
			Captain J.M.Cowan.	
			Lieut: F.J.Ward.	
			Lieut: H.Andrews.	
			Lieut: N.V.Kent.	
			Lieut: S.Keys.	
			Lieut: L.Rathbone.	
			Lieut: L.A.Kerr.	
			2/Lt: H.J.Bayliss.	
			2/Lt: I.A.Hildred.	
			2/Lt: J.Holland.	
			Captain A.W.Keeley. "D" Coy:	
			2/Lt: R.Shankland.	
			2/Lt: F.Bradley.	
			2/Lt: A.A.Lamb.	
			2/Lt: T.H.Quayle.	
			2/Lt: G.H.Cowherd.	
			2/Lt: T.W.Hall.	
			2/Lt: G.W.Gibson.	
			Captain E.R.Brittain. "E" Coy:	
			Lieut: J.O.Richardson.	
			2/Lt: G.Parsons.	
			2/Lt: H.M.Evans.	
			2/Lt: H.P.Firth.	
			Medical Officer. Capt Duke. R.A.M.C.	
			Warrant Officers:-	
			R.S.M. Cahill.	
			Army Schoolmaster Birkett.	
			C.S.M. Borland. "B" Coy:	
			C.S.M. Crooks. "D" Coy.	
			C.S.M.Gretton. "E" Coy.	
			Total number of O.R's proceeded overseas:- 756.	
			Battalion passes night in No.4. Rest Camp. Dunkirk.	

Army Form C. 2118.

WAR DIARY
or
INTELLIGENCE SUMMARY.
(Erase heading not required.)

Instructions regarding War Diaries and Intelligence Summaries are contained in F. S. Regs., Part II. and the Staff Manual respectively. Title pages will be prepared in manuscript.

Place	Date	Hour	Summary of Events and Information	Remarks and references to Appendices
DUNKIRK.	5.3.1919.		Battalion entrains at Sand Siding en route for Germany. Halts for meals made at Merris & Ghisenghien.	
	6.3.1919.		Journey through Belgium. Halts for meals at Huy, Charleroi & Verviers.	
	7.3.1919.		Battalion arrived at Beuel, near BONN, detrains and marches to Menden, where it is billeted, relieving the 10th (S) Bn. Argyle & Sutherland Highlanders. Battalion visited by Lt.Col. Forbes-Robertson, acting Brigadier, 97th Infantry Brigade.	
	8.3.1919.		Battalion attached to 97th Infantry Brigade, 32nd Division. Battalion settling into billets at Menden. Visit of Major General Lambert. (G.O.C. 32nd Division) and Lt.Col.Robinson. (A.A. & Q.M.G) Lieut: F.K.Ward. appointed Transport Officer. Lieut: N.V.Kent. -do- Lewis Gun Officer. 2/Lt: E.P.H.Pugh. -do- Intelligence & Civil Administration Officer.	
	9.3.1919.		Church Parade at Menden.	
	10.3.1919.		Battalion inspected on the Exerzier Platz, Hangelar, by General Sir.H.Plumer, Commanding 2nd Army.	
	11.3.1919.		Battalion training at Menden. Captain Duke. R.A.M.C. struck off the strength on proceeding to England.	
	12.3.1919.		Battalion training at Menden.	
	13.3.1919.		Battalion traing at Menden. Colonel A.C.Bolton holds Summary Court at Sieglar as Commandant, Sieglar Sub Area.	
	14.3.1919.		Practice Ceremonial Parade and training at Menden.	
	15.3.1919.		A Headquarters Company formed under supervision of Major A.G.Hills. The undermentioned Officers transferred to H.Q. Company for duty:-	
			Colonel A.C.Bolton.	
			Major A.G.Hills. Lieutl F.K.Ward. Lewis Gun Officer.	
			Capt; & Adjt: E.J.Lloyd. Lieut. N.V.Kent. Signalling Officer.	
			Lieut: H.E.Roose. Lieut: H.Andrews. Education Officer.	
			Lt; & Q.M.W.H.Smith. 2/Lt: H.J.Bayliss. Anti-Gas Officer.	
			2/Lt: E.P.H.Pugh. 2/Lt: T.H.Quayle.	
			Authority:-(B.R.O. No 50 of 15.3.19. para 10)	
			32nd Division renamed the Lancashire Division. Sir H.Jendwine assumes command of the Lancashire Division vice Major General Lambert.	

Army Form C. 2118.

WAR DIARY
or
INTELLIGENCE SUMMARY.

(Erase heading not required.)

Instructions regarding War Diaries and Intelligence Summaries are contained in F. S. Regs., Part II. and the Staff Manual respectively. Title pages will be prepared in manuscript.

Place	Date	Hour	Summary of Events and Information	Remarks and references to Appendices
MENDEN.	16.3.1919.		Church Parade in Menden Cinema.	
	17.3.1919.		2/Lt: H.J.Bayliss detached for duty 97th Infantry Brigade. Brigade Education Officer. Battalion Sports Committee formed.	
	18.3.1919.		The undermentioned Officers attached to the Unit from the 2nd Bn. Manchester Regt: Lieut: E.H.Murdock. Lieut: B.R.Cobley. 2/Lt: T.S.O'Grady. 2/Lt: J.D.O'Toole. 2/Lt: B.Burkett-Gottwaltz. 2/Lt: E.Hopkinson. 87 O.R's also transferred from the 2nd Bn. Manchester Regt:	
	19.3.1919.		Training at Menden. Football Match with 92nd Field Ambulance at Menden. won by 5 goals to 1. Colonel A.C.Bolton holds Summary Court at Sieglar.	
	20.3.1919.		Battalion training at Menden. Capt; Lee, R.A.M.C. taken on the strength. Battalion visited bt Major General Sir H.Jendwine.	
	21.3.1919.		Training at Menden. Battalion visited by Brigadier General A.Solly-Flood. Captain S.T.Brown, O.C. "B" Company admitted to Hospital.	
	22.3.1919.		Training at Menden.	
	23.3.1919.		Church Parade, Brigadier General Solly-Flood present.	
	24.3.1919.		Battalion training at Menden.	
	25.3.1919.		Battalion Training.	
	26.3.1919.		Battalion training.	
	27.3.1919.		Inspection of the Battalion by Brigadier General A.Solly-Flood.	
	28.3.1919.		Battalion Training.	
	29.3.1919.		"B" Company is moved to billets in Meindorf Village. Re-arrangements of all Battalion billets.	
	30.3.1919.		Arrival of Lt. Col. Traill CMG. DSO. 1st East Lancashire Regt. G.S.O.1. 3rd Division, to assume command of the Battalion.	

Lieut.-Col.
Commanding 53rd (Service)Battn.The Manchester Regt:

Army Form C. 2118.

WAR DIARY
or
INTELLIGENCE SUMMARY.
(Erase heading not required.)

Instructions regarding War Diaries and Intelligence Summaries are contained in F. S. Regs., Part II. and the Staff Manual respectively. Title pages will be prepared in manuscript.

Place	Date	Hour	Summary of Events and Information	Remarks and references to Appendices
MENDEN	March, 1919.		APPENDIX -o-o-o-o-o-o-o-o- Promotions made during the Month of March, 1919 88164 Sgt. Matthews, S.H. to be A/CSM 87675 A/Cpl Eady, C.R. to be A/Sgt. 88153 A/L-Cpl Mosby, N.S. to be A/Cpl -do- A/Cpl -do- L/Sgt 88170 A/Cpl Gettliffe, H. to be A/Sgt 88187 -do- Bodenham, F.L. -do- 251969 Sgt. Whitford, J.F. to be A/CQMS 25849 L/Sgt Baker, H. to be A/Sgt 88159 A/Cpl Harrison, A. -do- 88165 Cpl. Fotheringham, R. -do- 202418 A/Cpl Frickett, F. -do- 88176 -do- Kemp, R.E. -do- 52849 -do- Carter, C.J.R. to be L/Sgt 57314 -do- Worthington, W.J. -do- 62569 Cpl. Lynch, H.P. to be A/Sgt 88177 A/Cpl Lawrence, E.G. to be L/Sgt 87423 A/L-Cpl Donley, G. to be A/Cpl 87525 -do- Christian, J. -do- 87533 -do- Robertson, H. -do- 87401 -do- Cottam, J. -do- 60606 -do- Ribby B. -do- 78319 -do- Satterly, G.H. -do- 87691 -do- Wild, H. -do- 252631 -do- Carney, W.F. -do- 88173 -do- King, A. -do- 64144 -do- Pearson, W. -do- 78823 -do- Beavan, W. -do- 78280 -do- Gregory, E. -do-	

Army Form C. 2118.

WAR DIARY
or
INTELLIGENCE SUMMARY.
(Erase heading not required.)

Place: MENDEN
Date: March, 1919

Summary of Events and Information

APPENDIX (Continued)

```
79198   A/L-Cpl Nichols, A.      to be A/Cpl
57479    -do-   Fothergill, T.    -do-
87551   Pte    German, J.W.   to be A/L-Cpl
87380    "     Hewitt, V.         -do-
87535    "     Berry, W.          -do-
87541    "     Allen, T.E.        -do-
87464    "     Sharpeles, A.      -do-
87533    "     Dichairo, R.       -do-
87683   A/u.p./L-Cpl Mitchell, H.C. to be A/L-Cpl
87673    -do-   Howe, J.          -do-
88154    -do-   Merver, W.        -do-
87719    -do-   Lees, E.          -do-
87764    -do-   Jones, D.         -do-
87794    -do-   Tarbatt, G.W.     -do-
276769   -do-   Reed, T.          -do-
87964    -do-   Atherton, F.T. to be A/u.p./L-Cpl
88084   Pte    Robinson, S.       -do-
53193    "     Sugars, A.         -do-
87570    "     Graham, T.         -do-
87619    "     Thokpsnon, G.W.    -do-
87714    "     Pickthall, W.      -do-
87682    "     Marshall, F.       -do-
87668    "     Small, J.          -do-
87568    "     Holt, G.           -do-
79212    "     Kershaw, S.        -do-
78309    "     Stuart, J.         -do-
```

Army Form C. 2118.

WAR DIARY
or
INTELLIGENCE SUMMARY.
(Erase heading not required.)

Place	Date	Hour	Summary of Events and Information	Remarks and references to Appendices
MENDEN	March, 1919		APPENDIX (continued)	
			Revertions	
			87944 A/L-Cpl Berry, J. reverts to private	
			87953 -do- Holdsworth, J. -do-	
			87887 -do- Kelly, J. -do-	
			[signature]	
			Lieut.-Colonel,	
			Commanding 53rd (S) Battalion The Manchester Regiment.	

WAR DIARY
or
INTELLIGENCE SUMMARY.
(Erase heading not required.)

Army Form C. 2118.

53rd (service) Battalion The Manchester Regiment.
-o-o-o-o-o-o-o-o-o-o-o-o-o-

Place	Date	Hour	Summary of Events and Information	Remarks and references to Appendices
MENDEN.	April 1st.		The undermentioned Officers taken on strength of the Battalion and posted to Coys. shewn.	
			Major C.G.Moore. MC. "B" Company.	
			Lieut. F.H.Whitsmore. "D" "	
			Lieut. W.Bennett. "B" "	
			Lieut. J.N.Bernard. "B" "	
			2/Lt. H.Tucker. "D" "	
			Capt. R.M.File. "D" "	
			Companies renamed as follows:-	
			"B" Company to be "W" Company.	
			"A" " " "X" "	
			"B" " " "Y" "	
			"D" " " "Z" "	
	April 3rd.		Col. A.C.Bolton struck off the strength on proceeding to England. 2/Lt. I.A.Hildred and 2/Lt. G.W.Gibson struck off the strength on proceeding to England.	
	" 5th.		Lieut. L.Rathbone and 2/Lt R. Shankland admitted to Hospital.	
	" 9th.		Companies renamed as follows:-	
			"W" Company to be "C" Company.	
			"X" " " "A" "	
			"Y" " " "B" "	
			"Z" " " "D" "	
	" 10th.		Battalion route march. Lieut. R.P.Levy taken on strength of Battalion and posted to "B" Company.	

WAR DIARY
or
INTELLIGENCE SUMMARY.
(Erase heading not required.)

Army Form C. 2118.

Instructions regarding War Diaries and Intelligence Summaries are contained in F. S. Regs., Part II. and the Staff Manual respectively. Title pages will be prepared in manuscript.

Place	Date	Hour	Summary of Events and Information	Remarks and references to Appendices
MENDEN.	April 11th.		Lieut. F.Hammond and 2/Lt. H.P.Firth struck off the strength on proceeding to England. Capt. T.M.Cowan struck off the strength on proceeding for demobilisation.	
"	12th.		Capt. T.Browne, CF. is taken on the attached strength of the Battalion and posted to the "H.Q" Company.	
"	14th.		2/Lt. T.H.Quayle transferred from "D" Company to "C" Coy. Lieut. M.J.T.Fairman having reported to the Battalion from a course in England, is posted to "H.Q" Company as Education Officer.	
"	16th.		Lieut. L.R.Rathbone discharged Hospital.	
"	22nd.		Lieut. B.R.Cobley returned from leave.	
"	24th.		Major T.B.Lawrence, DSO. MC. DCM. taken on strength, Second in Command and posted to "H;Q" Coy.	
"	28th.		Battalion inspected by the Divisional Commander on Hargelar Exerzier Platz	
"	29th.		2/Lt. F.R.Ragg and 2/Lt. R. Shankland struck off the strength on proceeding to England. Capt. T.Rice G.F. taken on attached strength of the Battalion and posted to "H.Q" Coy.	
"	30th.		Major T.B.Lawrence, DSO. MC. DCM. struck off the strength on proceeding on transfer to the 51st Gordon Highlanders. Lieut. F.J.Ward admitted to Hospital. Lieut. S. Keys appointed acting Transport Officer vice Lieut. F.H. Ward.	

MENDEN:
1. 5. 19.

[signature]
Lt.-Colonel.
Commanding 53rd (service) Battalion The Manchester Regt.

Army Form C. 2118.

WAR DIARY
or
INTELLIGENCE SUMMARY.
(Erase heading not required.)

Instructions regarding War Diaries and Intelligence Summaries are contained in F. S. Regs., Part II. and the Staff Manual respectively. Title pages will be prepared in manuscript.

Place	Date	Hour	Summary of Events and Information	Remarks and references to Appendices
MINDEN. In Germany.			53rd (SERVICE) BATTN: THE MANCHESTER REGIMENT. -o-o-o-o-o-o-o-o-o-o-o-o-o-o-o-o-	
	1.5.1919.		Major. C.G.Moore, Capt: R.M.File, proceeded to England on demobilisation. Lieut: F.H.Whitamore assumes command of "B" Company, vice Major C.G.Moore. Lieut: J.F.Johnson proceeded to England on Educational Course.	
	4.5.1919.		Lieut: I.Rathbone transferred from "B" to "A" Company.	
	8.5.1919.		Battalion Route March. Lieut. M.V.Kent, leave to England.	
	12.5.1919.		Brigadier General A.Solly Flood, CB, CMG. DSO. assumed command of Brigade, vice Lt.-Colonel W.H.Traill, CMG. DSO. on his return from leave.	
	13.5.1919.		The Battalion inspected by the G.O.C.in C.(General Sir W.Robertson, GCB.KCVO.DSO.ADC.) at Hangelar Exerzier Platz.	
	16.5.1919.		"D" Company moved to MEINDORF, "B" Company moved to EMDEN. Capt: T.Browne, CF. leave to England.	
	17.5.1919.		Lieut: M.J.T.Fairman struck off the strength on proceeding for demobilisation.	
	21.5.1919.		Lieut: E.H.Murdoch rejoined from leave.	
	22.5.1919.		Lieut: E.H.Murdoch detached for duty at Divisional Headquarters. Lieut: G.B.Montgomery, 15th Bn. Lancashire Fusiliers, taken on strength and posted to "A" Coy.	
	24.5.1919.		Battalion Route March. 2/Lieut: J.D.O'Toole, leave to England.	

Army Form C. 2118.

WAR DIARY
or
INTELLIGENCE SUMMARY.
(Erase heading not required.)

Instructions regarding War Diaries and Intelligence Summaries are contained in F. S. Regs., Part II. and the Staff Manual respectively. Title pages will be prepared in manuscript.

Place	Date	Hour	Summary of Events and Information	Remarks and references to Appendices
			- SHEET 2 -	
MINDEN.	25.5.1919.		Lieut. F.J.Ward detached for duty as 3rd (Manchester) Inf. Brigade Transport Officer. Lieut. C.B.Montgomery appointed Battalion Transport Officer. 2/Lieut: J.N.Bernard, leave to U.K. Major A.K.D.Tillard taken on strength as Second in Command.	
	29.5.1919.		Lieut. J.C.Richardson, leave to U.K.	
	30.5.1919.		Lieut. H.Kelley, 51st Bn. Kings Liverpool Regt; taken on the strength and posted to "A" Coy. Lieut. E.M.Evans, leave to England. Lieut. N.V.Kent, rejoined from leave.	
	31.5.1919.		Battalion Route March.	
	1.6.1919.			

[signature]
Lieut.-Colonel.
Commanding 53rd (Service) Battn: The Manchester Regiment.

WAR DIARY
or
INTELLIGENCE SUMMARY.

(Erase heading not required.)

Form C. 2118.

Instructions regarding War Diaries and Intelligence Summaries are contained in F. S. Regs., Part II. and the Staff Manual respectively. Title pages will be prepared in manuscript.

Place	Date	Hour	Summary of Events and Information	Remarks and references to Appendices
			53rd (Service) Battalion Manchester Regiment. (contd)	
Germany	21.6.19.		Lt. Col. W.H.Trail rejoined from leave and assumed command of this battalion	
	22.6.19.		Lt. C. Parsons and Lt. L. Rathbone rejoin from leave.	
	23.6.19.		Lt. G. Parsons. admitted hospital.	
	24.6.19.		2nd Lt. O'Grady leave to U.K.	
	27.6.19.		~~Major V. Villard leave to U.K.~~ Lt. Col. Traill leave to U.K. Major A.K.D. Tillard assumes command of the battalion.	
	28.6.19.		Orders received that upon concentration cessation, battalion will relieve 51st Manchester Regt, at Birlinghoven and in line of control.	
	29.6.19.		Lt. Kerr leave to U.K.	
	3 .6.19.		Preparations for move to line of control	

A.K.D.Tillard. Major.
for Lt.Col.
Cmdg. 53rd (S) Bn. Manchester Regt

Army Form C. 2118.

WAR DIARY
or
INTELLIGENCE SUMMARY.
(Erase heading not required.)

Instructions regarding War Diaries and Intelligence Summaries are contained in F. S. Regs., Part II. and the Staff Manual respectively. Title pages will be prepared in manuscript.

Place	Date	Hour	Summary of Events and Information	Remarks and references to Appendices
			53rd (Service) Battn. Manchester Regt.	
Germany	1.6.19		Lt. C.B. Margrett posted to Unit as Education Officer.	
	3.6.19.		Half holiday in celebration of birthday of H.M. The King.	
	4.6.19.		Lieut. E.A.Crossley. M.C. joined this unit and posted to "A" Coy.	
	5.6.19.		Battalion route march.	
	8.6.19.		Lieut. J.F. Johnson. rejoins Unit from Educational Course at Newmarket. Capt. J.G.Lee. M.C. struck off strength on proceeding to England for demobilization.	
	9.6.19.		Lt. Colonel. Traill. leave to U.K. Major A.K.D. Tillard assumes command of Battalion. Lieut. J.W.Mann. R.A.M.C. appointed M.O. i/c Unit.	
	11.6.19.		Capt. E.R.Warton. leave to U.K. 2nd Lieut. J.M.Bernard rejoined from leave.	
	14.6.19.		Battalion route march. Lieut. Rathbone leave to U.K.	
	15.6.19.		Capt. H.J.Bayliss struck off strength of Unit as from 3.3.19. while performing duties of Brigade Education Officer.	
	19.6.19.		Battalion moves to Niederpleis in concentration of troops. Lt. Keys and 2nd Lt. J.P.O'Toole rejoin from leave.	
	2.6.19.		Lieut. F.Brady, and Lt. H. Andrews rejoin from leave.	

Army Form C. 2118.

WAR DIARY
or
INTELLIGENCE SUMMARY.
(Erase heading not required.)

Place	Date	Hour	Summary of Events and Information	Remarks and references to Appendices
BIRLINGHOVEN			**53rd (S) Bn. The Manchester Regt:**	
			Officers in the Battalion.	
			Commanding Officer. Lt.-Col W.H.Traill. CMG. DSO.	
			2nd in Command. Major A.K.D.Tillard.	
			Adjutant. Capt. E.J.Lloyd.	
			O.C. "A" Company. Capt. H.E.R.Warton.	
			O.C. "B" Company. Capt. H.Whitmore.	
			O.C. "C" Company. Capt. E.R.Brittain.	
			O.C. "D" Company. Capt. A.W.Keeley.	
	July 1st.		Battalion moved from NIEDER PLEIS to BIRLINGHOVEN and front line sector. Lieut. J.F.Johnson transferred from "A" Coy to "D" Company.	
	July 2nd.		Capt. H.E.R.Warton returned from leave. Lieut. G.Parsons discharged Hospital. The Brigade Cinema visited STIELDORF.	
	July 3rd.		Lieut. W.E.G.Serjeant. Leave to U.K.	
	July 4th.		Battalion Church Parade at RAUSCHENDORF.	
	July 5th.		Brigade Cinema visited STIELDORF.	
	July 7th.		2/Lt. B.Burkett Gottwaltz struck off strength on evacuation sick to England. "C" & "D" Companies commence firing G.M.C.	
	July 8th.		Lieut. H.E.Roose, leave to U.K.	
	July 9th.		Medical inspection of Battalion. Officers V Sergeants. Cricket Match. Lieut. L.Rathbone discharged Hospital.	

Army Form C. 2118.

WAR DIARY
or
INTELLIGENCE SUMMARY.
(Erase heading not required.)

Instructions regarding War Diaries and Intelligence Summaries are contained in F. S. Regs., Part II. and the Staff Manual respectively. Title pages will be prepared in manuscript.

Place	Date	Hour	Summary of Events and Information	Remarks and references to Appendices
BIRLINGHOVEN	July 9th.		Lieut. J.O. Richardson discharged Hospital.	
	July 11th.		Capt. H.G. Parker. RAMC reported as Medical Officer i/c.	
	July 12th.		2/Lt. T.S. O'Grady returned from leave.	
	July 13th.		Lt-Col W.H. Traill CMG. DSO. returned from leave.	
	July 14th.		Battalion Medical Inspection.	
	July 15th.		2/Lt. T.H. Quayle. returned from leave.	
	July 16th.		Medical inspection of Battalion.	
	July 17th.		"C" & "D" Companies complete firing G.M.C.	
	July 18th.		Lieut. L.A. Kerr returned from leave.	
	July 19th.		General Holiday, Peace Celebration.	
	July 20th.		"C" & "D" Companies relieve "A" & "B" Companies in outpost line. "A" & "B" Companies moved back to STIELDORF & RAUSCHENDORF respectively.	
	July 21st.		"A" & "B" Companies commence firing the G.M.C.	
	July 22nd.		Lieut. H. Kelly returned from leave.	
			Lieut. R.P. Levey assumed duty as Rail Control Officer, Freckwinkel, vice Lieut. Gower on leave.	
	July 25th.		Lieut. F. Bradley leave to U.K.	
			Transport inspected by Commanding Officer.	
			Lieut. H.E. Roose and Lieut. WEG. Serjeant returned from leave.	
	July 26th.		Lieut. & QM. W.H. Smith leave to U.K. 2/Lt. J.T. Milner to act as Quartermaster.	
			Capt. H.G. Parker RAMC, ceased to be attached to the Unit.	
	July 28th.		Brigade Concert Party visited STIELDORF.	
	July 30th.		Battalion Athletic Sports held at BIRLINGHOVEN.	

53RD (SERVICE) BN. THE MANCHESTER REGT.

Army Form C. 2118.

WAR DIARY
or
INTELLIGENCE SUMMARY.
(Erase heading not required.)

Instructions regarding War Diaries and Intelligence Summaries are contained in F. S. Regs., Part II. and the Staff Manual respectively. Title pages will be prepared in manuscript.

Place	Date	Hour	Summary of Events and Information	Remarks and references to Appendices
			53rd (Service) Bn. The Manchester Regiment.	
BIELINGHOVEN.	1.8.19.		Lieut. G.M.Margrett and 2/Lt T.H.Quayle transferred from "C" Company to "HQ" Company.	
	2.8.19.		Battalion Parade at STIELDORF at 08.55 hours. Conference of officers at STIELDORF, 1030 hours. Capt. E.R.Brittain proceeded on leave to U.K.	
	4.8.19.		Lieut. N.V.Kent returned from special continental leave Military Training suspended owing to Bank Holiday. Battalion receives orders to take over Right Battn: Sector of Eastern Divisional Forward Area on 5.8.19	
HENNEF.	5.8.19.		Battalion takes over HENNEF Sector of Eastern Division al Front, being located as follows:- "HQ" Company. HENNEF. "A" " Factory HENNEF. "B" " BRÖL. "C" " EISCHEID. "D" "	
	6.8.19.		Lieut. A.A.Lamb proceeded on leave to U.K.	
	7.8.19.		Lieut. L.T.Smith leave to U.K. Lieut. F.Bradley returned from leave. Lt.-Col W.H.Traill CMG.DSO, assumes command of the 3rd (Manchester) Inf. Brigade vice Major General Solly-Flood CB.CMG.DSO. on leave. Major A.K.D.Tillard assumes command of the Battalion. T/Lieut F.H.Whitamore, West Yorks Regt to be acting Captain while in command of a Company.(Authy. Divnl: List No 12 A.556) Capt. E.J.Lloyd leave to U.K. Lieut. H.E.Roose to be Acting Adjutant. Lieut. H.M.Evans admitted Hospital.	
	8.8.19.		Capt.D Hearne RAMC, taken on strength and posted "HQ" Co.	

Army Form C. 2118.

WAR DIARY
or
INTELLIGENCE SUMMARY.
(Erase heading not required.)

Instructions regarding War Diaries and Intelligence Summaries are contained in F. S. Regs., Part II. and the Staff Manual respectively. Title pages will be prepared in manuscript.

Sheet -2-

Place	Date	Hour	Summary of Events and Information	Remarks and references to Appendices
HENNEF.	10.8.19		Lieut. & Q.M. W.H. Smith returned from leave.	
	13.8.19		Capt. F.H. Whitamore proceeded on leave to U.K.	
			2/Lt. A.E. Owen having reported to Chinese Labour Corps Depot, is struck off the strength.	
	14.8.19		Lieut. H. Kelley returned from leave.	
	15.8.19		Lieut. H. Andrews proceeded on leave to U.K.	
			Capt. D.H. Hearne, RAMC, is struck off the strength.	
			Lieut. J.N. Gale RAMC, is taken on the strength and posted to "HQ" Company.	
	16.8.19		Lieut. L. Rathbone, leave to U.K.	
			Major T. Browne C.F. having reported to Divisional H.Q. for duty is struck off the strength.	
			Capt. R.E. Scantlebury C.F. is taken on the strength.	
			Lieut. G.M. Evans discharged hospital.	
	17.8.19		Capt. E.R. Brittain returned from leave.	
	18.8.19		Lieut. G. Parsons leave to U.K.	
	19.8.19		Lieut. J. Holland rejoined from leave.	
	20.8.19		Lieut. J.F. Johnson leave to U.K.	
	21.8.19		Lieut. W. Bennett rejoined from leave.	
	22.8.19		2/Lt. H. Tucker leave to U.K.	
			Lieut. H. Kelley detailed for duty as Rail Control Officer, FRECKWINKEL.	
	23.8.19		Lieut. L.M. Smith rejoined from leave.	
			Lieut. E.A. Crossley MC leave to U.K.	
			Lieut. A.A. Lamb rejoined from leave.	
	24.8.19		Capt. A.W. Keeley leave to U.K.	
	25.8.19		Lieut. B.R. Cobley MC. leave to U.K.	
	26.8.19		Lieut. A.A. Lamb detailed for duty with D.A.P.M. SIEGBURG, MULLDORP.	
			Lieut. W. Hall rejoined from leave.	

Army Form C. 2118.

WAR DIARY
or
INTELLIGENCE SUMMARY.
(Erase heading not required.)

Instructions regarding War Diaries and Intelligence Summaries are contained in F. S. Regs., Part II. and the Staff Manual respectively. Title pages will be prepared in manuscript.

Place	Date	Hour	Summary of Events and Information	Remarks and references to Appendices
			Sheet 3.	
			=======	
HENNEP.	27.8.19.		Capt. R.E.Scantlebury, leave to U.K.	
	28.8.19.		Lieut. C.B.Montgomery MC, leave to U.K.	
	30.8.19.		T-2/Lt. D.D.O'Toole to be T/Lieut from 30.7.19. Lieut. R.P.Levey leave to U.K.	
	2.9.19.			

An. A. Tihard Major.
Commanding 53rd (S) Bn. Manchester Regt

Army Form C. 2118.

WAR DIARY
or
INTELLIGENCE SUMMARY.
(Erase heading not required.)

Instructions regarding War Diaries and Intelligence Summaries are contained in F. S. Regs., Part II. and the Staff Manual respectively. Title pages will be prepared in manuscript.

Place	Date	Hour	Summary of Events and Information	Remarks and references to Appendices
HENNEF.			**53rd (Service) Battn. The Manchester Regiment.**	
			H.Q. OFFICERS OF THE UNIT.	
			Commanding Officer. Lieut. Col.W.H.TRAILL: CMG. DSO.	
			2nd in Command. Major. A.K.D.TILLARD.	
			Adjutant. Capt. H.E.ROOSE.	
			Asst. Adjutant. Lieut. E.P.H.PUGH.	
			Quartermaster. Lieut. & Q.M. W.H.SMITH.	
	Sept. 1st.		Capt. E.H.Lloyd returned from leave.	
	2nd.		Lieut. G.M.Margrett leave to U.K.	
			Battalion Sergeants Mess established at HENNEF.	
			Lieut. G.Parsons returned from leave.	
	3rd.		Commanding Officer's Inspection of Headquarters and "D" Company.	
			Capt. E.J.Lloyd assumes Command of "D" Company - vice Capt. A.W.Keeley.	
	4th.		Battalion proceeds on Rhine Steamer up to COBLENZE.	
			Major A.K.D.Tillard leave to U.K.	
			Capt. E.R.Brittain assumes command of the Battalion. vice Major A.K.D.Tillard; Lieut. Col. Traill.CMG.DSO. being in temporary command of the 3rd Manchester Infantry Brigade.	
			Lieut. H.Andrews returned from leave.	
			Capt. F.H.Whitamore returned from leave.	
	5th.		Lieut. J.F.Johnson rejoined from leave.	
			2/Lieut. H.Tucker rejoined from leave.	
	7th.		Capt. A.W.Keeley rejoined from leave.	
			Lieut. A.E.Crossley rejoined from leave.	

Army Form C. 2118.

WAR DIARY
or
INTELLIGENCE SUMMARY.
(Erase heading not required.)

Instructions regarding War Diaries and Intelligence Summaries are contained in F. S. Regs., Part II. and the Staff Manual respectively. Title pages will be prepared in manuscript.

Place	Date	Hour	Summary of Events and Information	Remarks and references to Appendices
HENNEF.	Sept. 8th.		Battalion Parade held at 0745 hours and to beheld daily in future. 2/Lieut. J.N.Bernard leave to U.K. Capt. S.T.Brown and Lieut. F.J.Lloyd Ward having been evacuated to Base Sick on 25.3.19. and 7.7.19. respectively are struck off the strength from those dates. (Authy - Rhine Army No. A912/51(01))	
"	10th.		Capt. H.E.R.Warton, Lieut. W.E.G.Sergeant, and 2/Lieut. K.Frost struck off the strength on proceeding for demobilization. Lieut. J.F.Johnson assumes command and pay of "A" Coy. from 10.9.19. vice Capt. H.E.R.Warton.	
"	11th.		Capt. T.Rice CF leave to UK. Lieut. C.B.Montgomery MC rejoined from leave. Capt. Scantlebury CF rejoined from leave. Lieut. B.R.Cobley MC having assumed duties of Brigade Intelligence Officer is struck off the strength except for record purposes.	
"	13th.		Major General A.Solly Flood CB,CMG, DSO assumes command of the 3rd Manchester Inf. Bde vice. Lieut.Col. W.H.TRAILL. CMG.DSO. Lieut. Col. W.H.Traill. CMG. DSO assumes Command of the Battalion vice. Capt. E.R.Brittain. Lieut. H.M.Evans proceeded to COLOGNE Deutsch Station for duty under R.T.O.	
"	14th.		Lieut. R.P.Levy rejoined from leave.	
"	17th.		Capt. A.W.Keeley struck off the strength on proceeding for demobilization.	
"	16th.		Lieut. H.E.Roose confirmed an appointment of Adjutant and granted acting rank of Captain.	
"	18th.		2/Lieut. H.Tucker. struck off the strength on proceeding for demobilization. Lieut. Margrett rejoined from leave.	
"	24th.		Brigade Sports held at HENNEF. 2/Lieut. K.A.J.N.Bernard rejoined from leave,	

Army Form C. 2118.

WAR DIARY
or
INTELLIGENCE SUMMARY.
(Erase heading not required.)

Instructions regarding War Diaries and Intelligence Summaries are contained in F. S. Regs., Part II. and the Staff Manual respectively. Title pages will be prepared in manuscript.

Place	Date	Hour	Summary of Events and Information	Remarks and references to Appendices
HENNEF.	24th Sept.		Lieut. H.Kelley having rejoined from detachment is posted to "B" Coy.	
	26th	"	Lieut. H.M.Evans. struck off the strength.	
	27th	"	Major A.K.D.Tillard rejoined from leave.	
	30th.	"	Reorganisation of the Battalion on a three Company Basis i.e. two fighting Companies, one H.Q. reserve Company. Officers re-distributed as follows;—	

H.Q.

Lieut.Col. W.H.Traill CMG DSO.   C.O.
Major A.K.D.Tillard.   2nd in Command.
Capt. H.E.Roose.   Adjutant.
Lieut. E.P.H.Pugh.   Asst. Adjt.
Lieut. & Q.M. W.H.Smith.   Quartermaster.

"A" Company. (Reserve Coy.)

Lieut. J.F.Johnson.
Lieut. N.V.Kent.   (Lewis Gun Officer).
Lieut. H.Andrews.   (Signal Officer)
Lieut. Montgomery. M.C.   (Transport Officer)
Lieut. J.T.Milner.   (Messing Officer)
2/Lieut. T.H.Quayle.   (Sports Officer)
Lieut. S.Keys.
2/Lieut. J.N.Bernard.

"B" Coy. (1st Fighting Coy.)

Capt. F.H.Whitmore.
Lieut. R.P.Levy.
Lieut. L.A.Kerr.
Lieut. W.Bennet.
Lieut. L.Rathbone.
Lieut. J.Holland.
Lieut. A.E.Crossley. MC. (Education Officer).

"C" Company (2nd Fighting Coy.)

Capt. E.R.Brittein.
Capt. E.J.Lloyd.
Lieut. L.T.Smith.
Lieut. F.Bradley.
Lieut. J.O.Richardson.
Lieut. W.Hall.
Lieut. G.Parsons.
Lieut. G.M.Margrett (Education Officer)

Lieut. Col.
Commdg. 53RD (SERVICE) BN. THE MANCHESTER REGT.

Army Form C. 2118.

WAR DIARY
or
INTELLIGENCE SUMMARY.
(Erase heading not required.)

Instructions regarding War Diaries and Intelligence Summaries are contained in F. S. Regs., Part II. and the Staff Manual respectively. Title pages will be prepared in manuscript.

Place	Date	Hour	Summary of Events and Information	Remarks and references to Appendices
Hennef			53rd.(Service)Bn.Manchester Regiment	
			Officers of the Battalion.	
			Commanding Officer Lieut. Col. W.H. Traill CMG. DSO.	
			2nd in Command Major A.K.D. Tillard.	
			Adjutant Capt. H.E. Roose.	
			O.C. "A" Coy. Lieut. H.E. Johnson.	
			O.C. "B" Coy. Capt. H.F. Whitamore.	
			O.C. "C" Coy. Capt. E.R. Brittain.	
			O.C. "D" Coy. Capt. E.J. Lloyd.	
			=0=0=0=0=0=0=0=0=0=0=0=0=0=0=	
	October 1.		2/Lieut. J.N. Bernard proceeded to B.H.Q. as Sigs. Officer.	
	October 2.		Battn. Lewis Gun Class commenced	
	October 4.		Redistribution of Officers of the Battalion. Lieut. Pugh.) proceeded to B.H.Q. as Civil Administrator	
	October 6.		Football Match Battn. Team versus Officers and Sergeants.	
	October 8.		Reveille at 0615 hours and Retreat at 1730 hours.	
	October 9.		53rd Manchesters versus 52nd Manchesters Football	
			Lieut. Levy admitted into Hospital. Rev. Scantlebury to Military Prison Siegburg.	
	October 10.		Lecture on War Savings at the Y.M.C.A.	
	October 11.		Brigade Horse Show.	
	October 13.		Major A.G. Hills struck off. Strength.	
	October 17.		Lieut. W. Hall to Aldershot Gas Course Lieut. H. Kelly. proceeded for Demob.	

Army Form C. 2118.

WAR DIARY
or
INTELLIGENCE SUMMARY.
(Erase heading not required.)

Instructions regarding War Diaries and Intelligence Summaries are contained in F.S. Regs., Part II. and the Staff Manual respectively. Title pages will be prepared in manuscript.

Place	Date	Hour	Summary of Events and Information	Remarks and references to Appendices
HENNEF.	October 20.		Lieut. J.O. Richardson proceeded to U.K. (Manchester) for Regimental Flag.	
	October 22.		Lieuts L.T. Smith L. Rathbone W. Bennett proceeded to Concentration Camp for Demob.	
	October 23.		Capt. Whitamore and Lieut. Pugh. proceeded to Concentration Camp for Demob.	
	October 24.		The Battalion is disbanded, and transferred to 51st and 52nd Battns. Manchester Regt.	

Walsh
Capt.,
Commanding Details 53rd (Service) Battn. Manchester Regt.
4.11.19.

www.ingramcontent.com/pod-product-compliance
Lightning Source LLC
Chambersburg PA
CBHW081505160426
43193CB00014B/2595